JAZZ philharmonic *Second Set*

✛ making jazz easy in the string orchestra

randy sabien & bob phillips

Alfred Publishing Co., Inc.
16320 Roscoe Blvd., Suite 100
P.O. Box 10003
Van Nuys, CA 91410-0003
alfred.com

23187 (Book) ISBN-10: 0-7390-3621-1
ISBN-13: 978-0-7390-3621-1

26308 (Book/CD) ISBN-10: 0-7390-4421-4
ISBN-13: 978-0-7390-4421-6

randy sabien

As a fourth grader in Rockford, Illinois, Randy dreamed of playing drums in a rock and roll band. At the same time, his drum and orchestra leader, Don Zimmerman, dreamed of building up the string section in the school orchestra. Soon Randy found himself studying violin with Hannah Armstrong—a relationship that would last until he left for college in 1974. At the University of Illinois, the world of etudes, concertos and symphonies merged with the world of pop music, garage bands and electric guitars through the medium of improvised jazz.

Randy currently performs with the Fiddle-head Band featuring legendary drummer Clyde Stubblefield, a Tribute to Stephane Grappelli with bassist Brian Torff (Grappelli alumni), and as a special guest with Corky Siegel's Chamber Blues. Randy has played folk music with Rock and Roll Hall of Fame inductee Jim Post, Mimi Farina, Kate Wolf and Greg Brown, and has appeared on the Prairie Home Companion radio show and PBS's Austin City Limits. To his credit are several critically acclaimed recordings on his own label. A pioneer in jazz education, he founded the string department at Berklee College of Music in 1978, and has conducted jazz clinics for thousands of string students and teachers, including the International String Workshops in Europe. Randy currently resides in Hayward, WI. To contact him about performances, workshops or recordings, check out his website at www.randysabien.com.

bob phillips

With over 25 years of experience in a public school classroom, as well as over 15 years as a teacher trainer, Bob brings a wealth of knowledge and experience to arranging alternative music for the string classroom. An expert in the use of folk fiddling and jazz in the string orchestra, Bob is renowned both as an innovator in string education and as a leader in the alternative styles movement. His students have been successful in many aspects of the music world, including both classical and alternative styles.

Bob is also known for his strategies for large group heterogeneous beginning string instruction, and for the use of technology in the classroom. He taught for 27 years in Saline, MI building a string program with over 700 students (considered to be a model of excellence in both classical and alternative music) before starting a new program in Tecumseh, MI. He is the co-author of the *String Explorer, Fiddlers Philharmonic* and *Jazz Philharmonic* series of books, is a composer of school performance music, and is the founder of the Saline Fiddlers Philharmonic. Bob has conducted many youth symphonies, honors and all-state orchestras and camps. He was selected as Teacher of the Year nine times by various professional organizations and, with his wife Pam, as Saline's Citizens of the Year for their role in arts education and management in the community.

table of contents

The Groove Goes On (G Major, Swing, 12-bar blues) 4

Highway Boogie (C Major, Blues, 8-bar shuffle). 7

South of the Border (G Major, Latin, AAB form) 10

In a Funk (A Major, Blues Rock, 8 bars) 13

Return to Whatever (A minor, Latin, 16 bars) 16

The Boy Is Blue (G minor, Swing, 12-bar blues) 19

Play It Cool (A minor, Swing, 12-bar blues) 22

Taking It Slow (C Major, Ballad, 8 bars) .25

Minor Incident (A minor, Rock waltz, AAB) 28

Who's the Bossa? (C, F, E♭ Major, Bossa, AABA) 32

Boppin' Along (E minor, Medium swing, 16 bars) 38

introduction

The world of string playing is changing. Alternative styles of music are being played by musicians of all ages, nationwide. The jazz string program at Berklee College, started by Randy Sabien, now boasts 120 students. At the American String Teacher's Association National Convention in 2003 and at the ASTA Forum in 2004, well over 75 sessions were devoted to alternative styles of music. By embracing the overwhelming similarities and bonds between string players, and acknowledging the real differences of style, barriers between musicians are breaking down. Around the country, school ensembles playing jazz and fiddle music are becoming commonplace. Three of the finalists and two of the winners at the ASTA 2003 Alternative Styles Competition studied with Randy and Bob, and used *Jazz Philharmonic* materials. Both Randy and Bob have been at the forefront of the alternative styles explosion, and now further explore the worlds of jazz and improvisation in *Jazz Philharmonic: Second Set*. *Jazz Philharmonic: Second Set* builds from simple tunes, to more complex ones. In a pedagogically tested sequence, improvisation exercises build from very simple concepts to multiple-key changes and challenging rhythms.

The layout of the book includes a Preparatory Page for each tune. Echo back each phrase Randy plays on the CD to develop a sense of jazz style and timing. Mastery of the Preparatory Page building blocks will prepare you to play the tunes, add solos and begin improvising. New in *Jazz Philharmonic: Second Set* are improvisation tips—it's just like having a private lesson on each tune! The Tune Page includes background parts for the violins and violas while the cellos and basses also learn to play jazz bass lines. The Solos Page introduces two progressively difficult jazz solos based on the tune. Developing arrangements is easy; some students can play the tune while others play a background or bass part. Individuals or sections can take turns playing the written-out solos, as well as improvising new solos. Easy piano parts are included in the teacher's manual so a complete rhythm section can be added to the strings. If no rhythm section is available, the CD can be used in performance. The left channel features Randy performing all the written tunes, solos, and several choruses of improvisation. The right channel features a professional rhythm section playing all the Background 2 and Bass 2 parts. By panning right or left you can play along with Randy or the rhythm section. The CD creates a great avenue for beginning improvisation as well as playing some great jazz tunes.

Put on the CD, learn the tunes and play along with Randy and the band. Enjoy!

the groove goes on   tune and background

the groove goes on solos

the groove goes on **preparatory page**

CD: Like many jazz tunes, the blues scale is the source for a simple riff repeated over the standard 12-bar blues chord progression. This tune uses only three notes, but check out "Bag's Groove," by Milt Jackson on the Modern Jazz Quartet's "European Concert" recording to hear a melody using more of the scale. **Improvisation Tip:** Use the G blues scale for the entire tune: slide into the "blue" notes (B♭, D♭, F) and into the root (G). Play a short phrase, then rest. Play the same phrase again and rest again. Remember, rest and repetition are your friends!

track **two**

highway boogie **preparatory page**

CD: This is a chord progression based on the Big Bill Broonzy tune "Key to the Highway." The accompaniment is a chunky shuffle rhythm created by the solo-guitar playing of such roots musicians as Broonzy, Robert Johnson and Tampa Red. **Improvisation Tip:** Once again the blues scale is going to get you through the entire tune. The "blue" notes here are E♭, G♭ and B♭. Release the pressure from the fingers of the left hand and glide into these notes. Don't be afraid to dig into the string with the bow and get a rough, gritty sound—much like the sound of the singers who created this powerful, soulful music.

track **four**

highway boogie tune and background

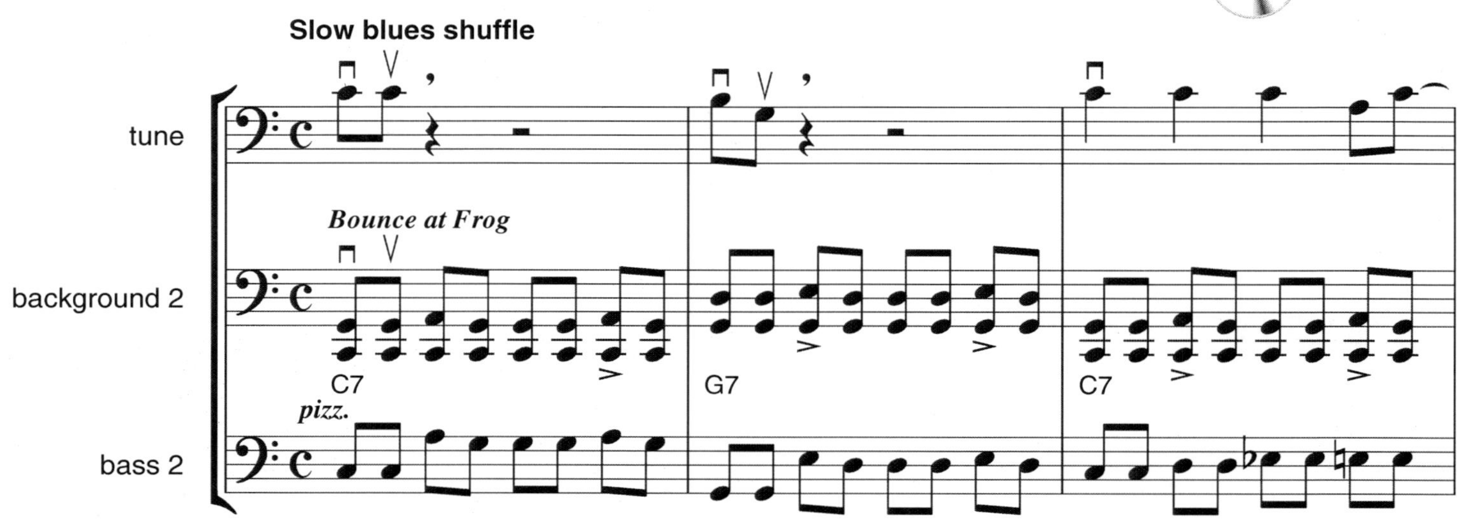

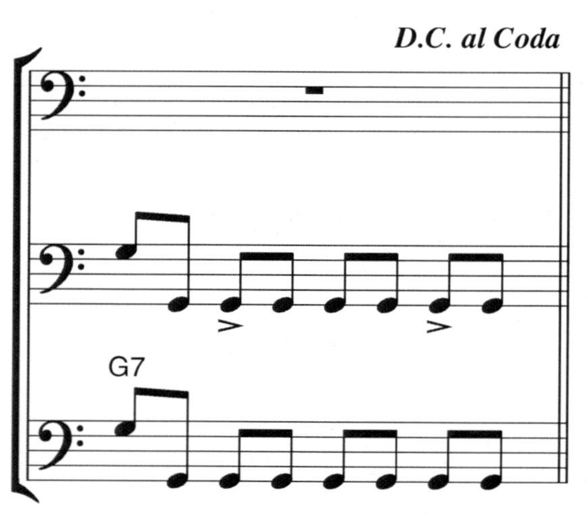

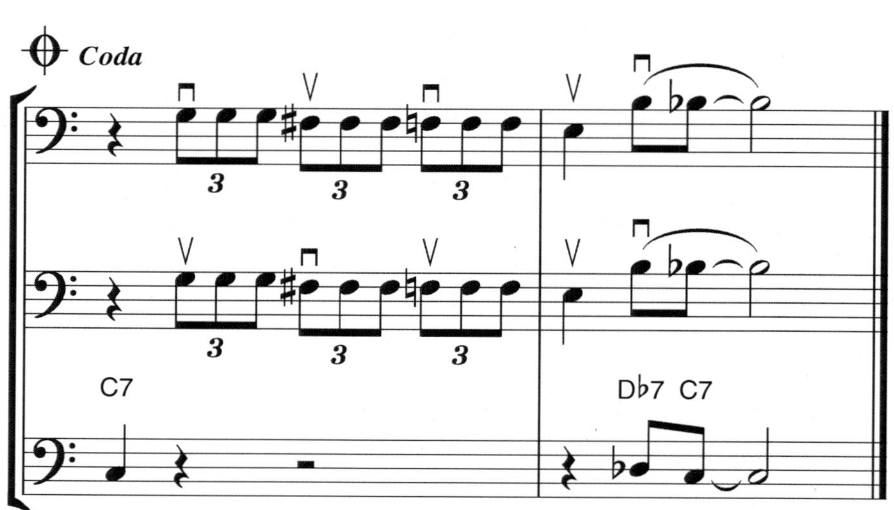

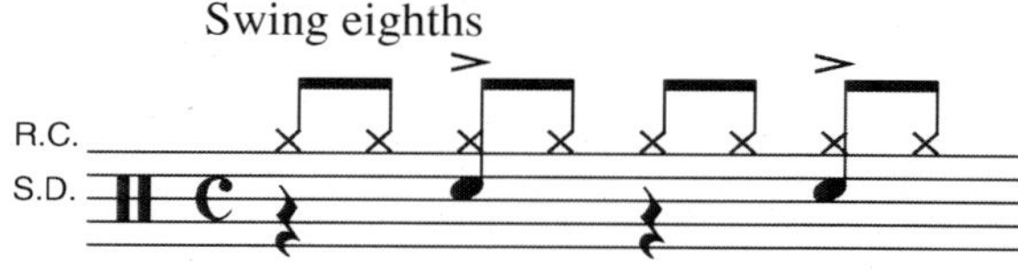

highway boogie solos

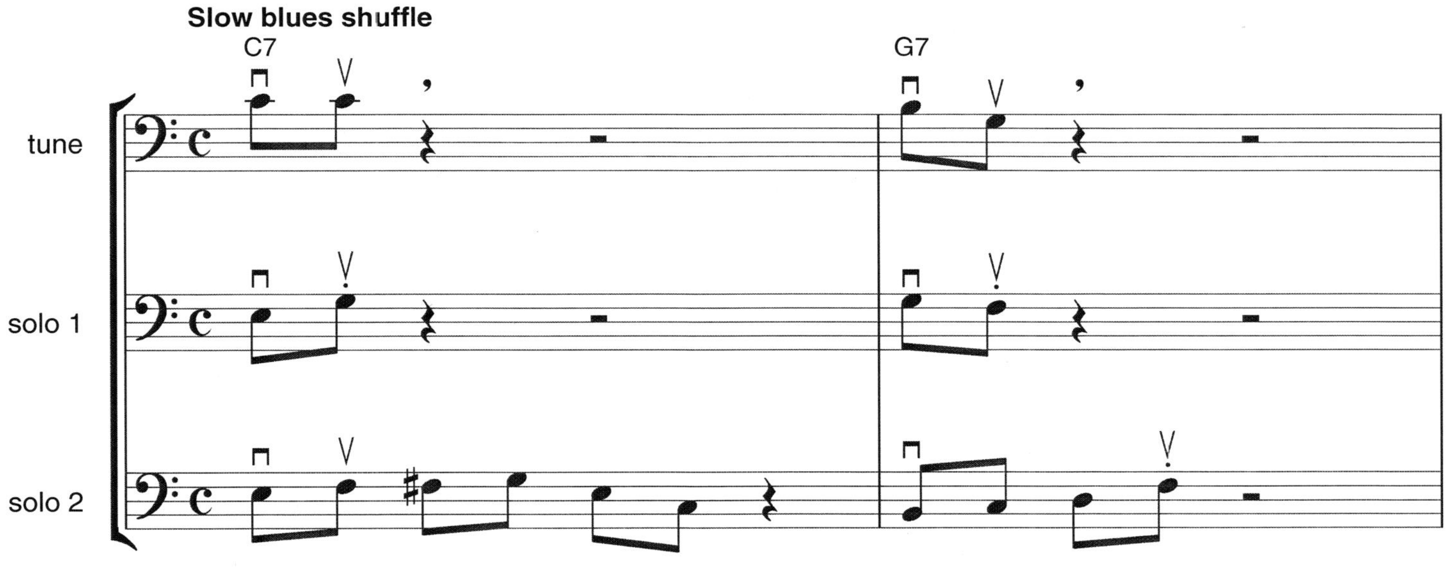

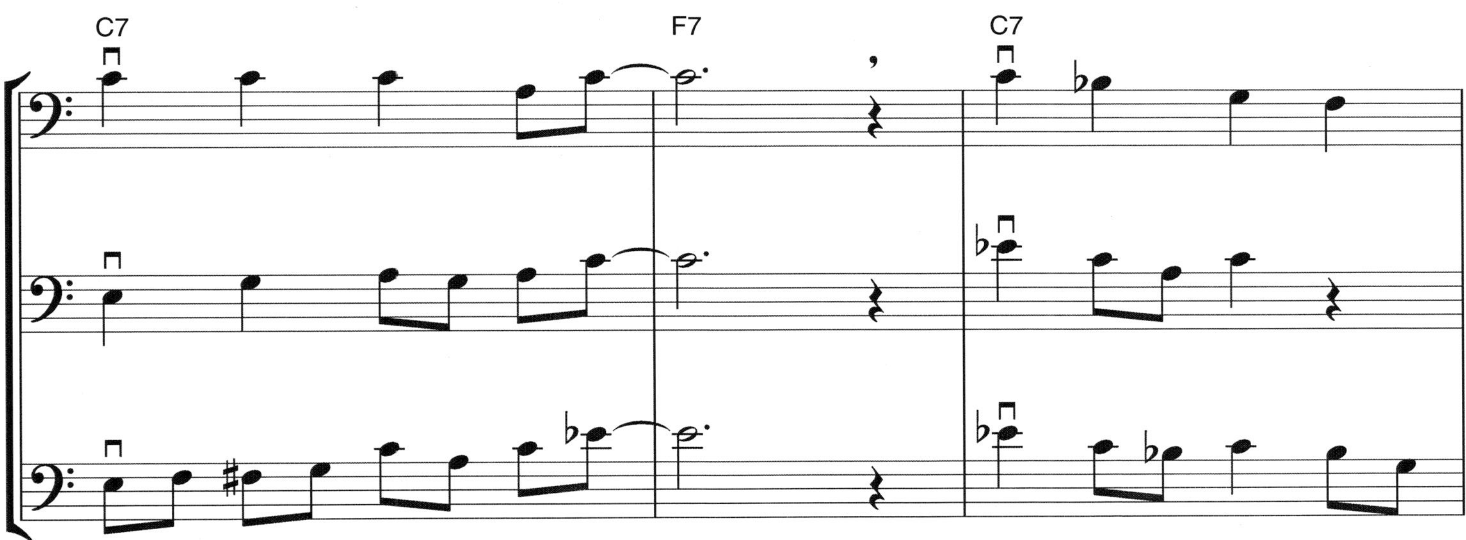

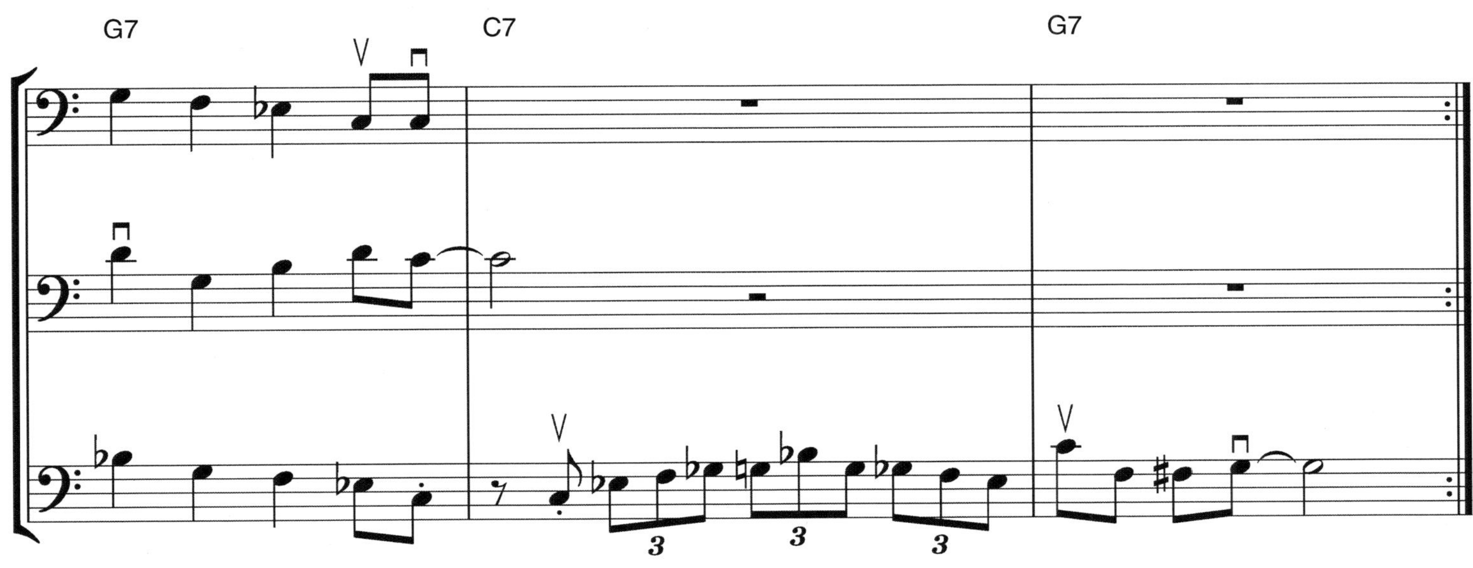

south of the border tune and background

south of the border solos

south of the border preparatory page

CD: Latin styles use "straight" or even eighth notes. In this tune, there are many syncopated (off-beat) eighth notes that should be played very short. A standard Latin-jazz tune is "Blue Bossa," by trumpeter Kenny Dorham. Joe Henderson has a well-respected recording of it on Blue Note. **Improvisation Tip:** A "be-bop" scale uses both the naturally occurring seventh note of a major scale (F♯ in the key of G) and the lowered seventh (F♮ in the key of G). Notice that the chords in the first half of the tune move back and forth between Gmaj7 (G triad with an F♯) and Fmaj7 (F triad with an E♮). The G after the F chord means the bass plays a G against it giving it a suspenseful, unresolved sound. Use F♯ in your melody for the G and drop it down to F♮ for the F. That's the only adjustment you need to make to play the changes.

track **six**

in a funk preparatory page

CD: Funk is a powerful style of rock music made famous by James Brown, Tower of Power and Earth, Wind and Fire and fused into jazz by Herbie Hancock, Miles Davis, the Crusaders and contemporary groups such as Medeski, Martin and Wood. Watch the film "Standing in the Shadows of Motown" to see how a group of rhythm-section musicians known as the Funk Brothers created the music behind such singers as Smokey Robinson and Marvin Gaye. You are playing along with one of the legendary innovators of funk from the 60's…Clyde Stubblefield. **Improvisation tip:** Use the A scale to create a long, soaring melody or start cookin' by using 16th notes. The blues scale can work through the B^7 chord or acknowledge it by using a D♯.

track **eight**

in a funk tune and background

track **nine**

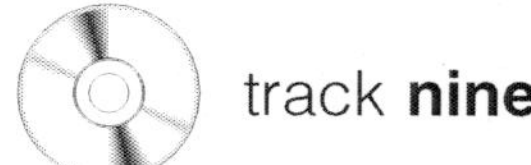

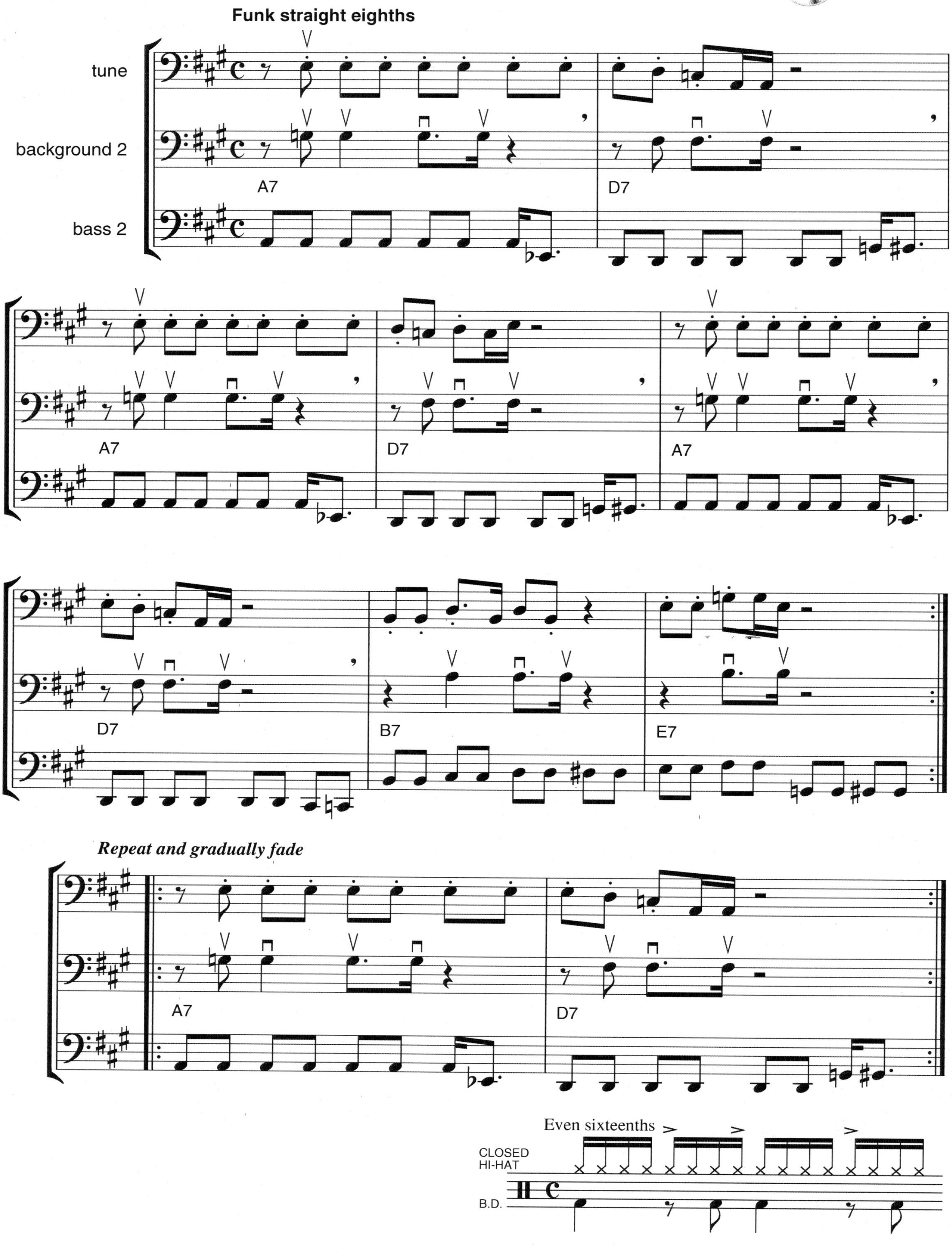

in a funk solos

return to whatever tune and background

Latin straight eighths

tune

background 2

bass 2

Am7

G7

Fmaj7

E7

Am7

G7

Fmaj7

E7

Am

E7

Am

Even eighths

CLOSED HI-HAT

RIM

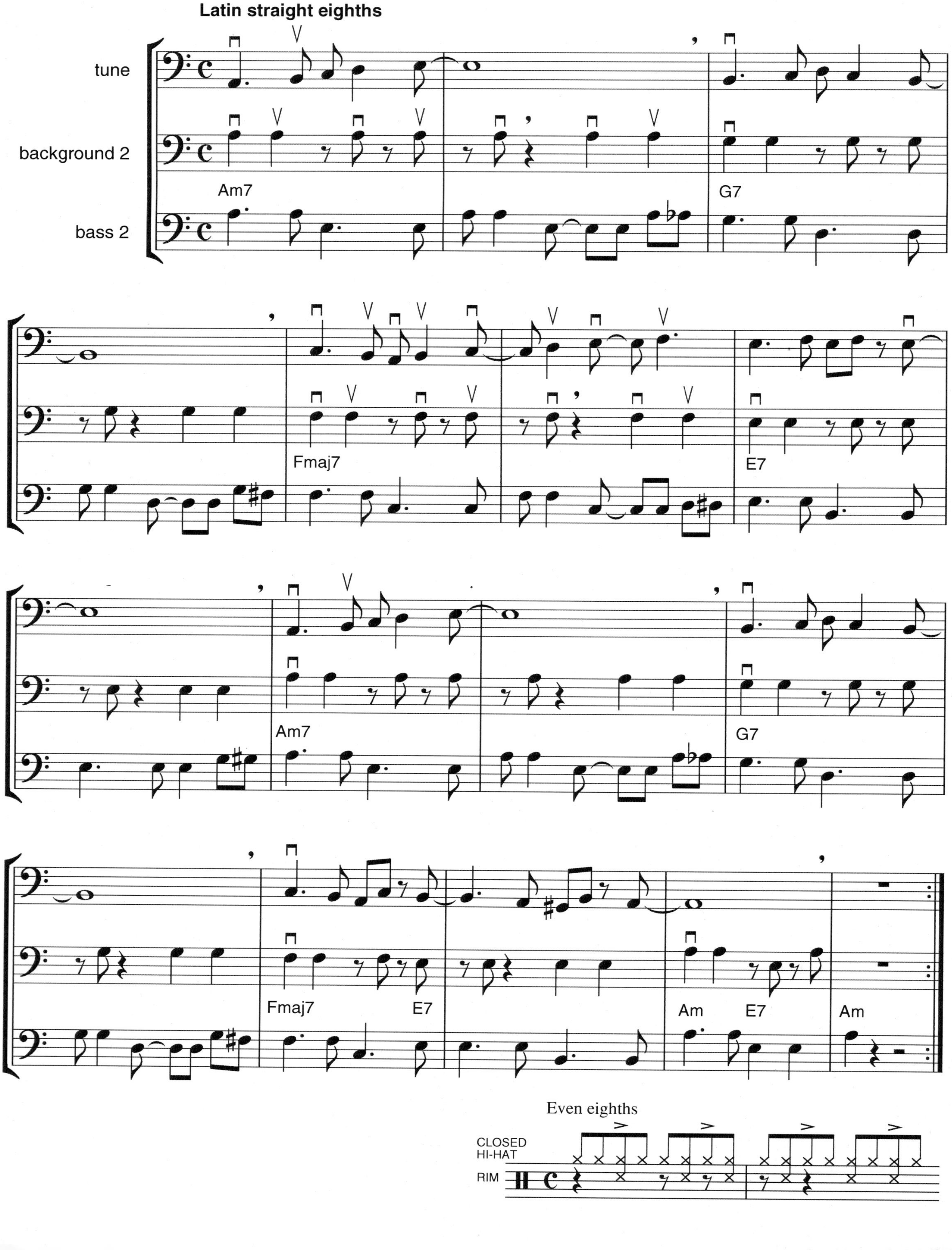

return to whatever solos

return to whatever preparatory page

CD: Dizzy Gillespie was a strong advocate for integrating Latin and/or Afro-Cuban styles into jazz. His 1948 album, "Dizzy Gillespie Big Band in Concert," featuring Cuban drummer Chano Pozo, helped launch the popularity of this rich and evocative music. Contemporary musicians continue this practice. Ry Cooder, for example, has done this with his recordings of the Cuban group "Buena Vista Social Club." **Improvisation Tip:** The chord progression follows the scale down from the root: A, G, F and E. Any form of an A minor scale will work as well as the blues scale. A melody using long notes on a low string will give a romantic or haunting feeling, while a more active melody using eighth notes on higher strings will create an exciting, energetic mood.

track **ten**

A Minor "be-bop" Scale

One-Bar Rhythmic Echoes

Two-Bar Rhythmic Echoes

One-Bar Melodic Echoes

Two-Bar Melodic Echoes

the boy is blue preparatory page

CD: Hard driving shuffle blues are part of the backbone of all contemporary music. Check out the classic, "Green Onions," as played by Booker T. and the MGs.

Improvisation Tip: Having the entire band rest on the last measure every time gives a space for "solo pickups." The first notes of Solo 1 belong to measure 12. When you improvise a solo, try making up your own solo pickups to fill measure 12. Solo 2 starts each phrase with the root of the chord. Try this idea when you improvise so you can begin "playing to the changes." That means only looking at the chord symbols or memorizing them to find material for improvising.

track **twelve**

When a phrase ends on a syncopated beat, such as the "and" of 4, it is an anticipation of the next beat. Even though it looks like it belongs to the measure it is written in, it feels like beat 1 of the next measure.

the boy is blue
tune and background

the boy is blue solos

play it cool tune and background

track **fifteen**

play it cool solos

play it cool preparatory page

CD: This tune uses the "call and response" device. One group of instruments plays a riff and another group answers back with a different one. "Moanin," by Bobby Timmons (recorded by Art Blakey), or "So What," by Miles Davis (on his Kind of Blue recording), are just two examples to listen to. **Improvisation Tip:** This is another 12-bar blues, but it has a little twist to it in measure 9. Instead of going directly to the V chord as you might expect, it goes to the chord a half step above (F^7) first, and then resolves down to the V chord (E^7) in the next bar. You can acknowledge this event by arpeggiating the chord as in Solo 2.

track **fourteen**

taking it slow   preparatory page

CD: Jazz violinist Stephane Grappelli was a genius at interpreting ballads. Listen to his versions of the Django Reinhardt classic "Nuages," or his duo album, "Talk of the Town," with pianist Alan Clare. **Improvisation Tip:** Notice in measure 6 of Solo 1 that the note B♭ appears against an A⁷ chord. A⁷ functions as the V chord of D and wants to move to the D minor chord in the next bar. Since the D harmonic minor scale includes a B♭, including it on the A⁷ prepares us to move into that tonality. Solo 2 uses a rhythmic effect called "double-time feel." By using 16th notes, it sounds like the tune is going twice as fast, but the rhythm section holds the original tempo steady underneath. Be sure to swing the 16ths.

track **sixteen**

*Notice how including the "blues" 3rd (E♭) changes the mood of the melody.

taking it slow tune and background

track **seventeen**

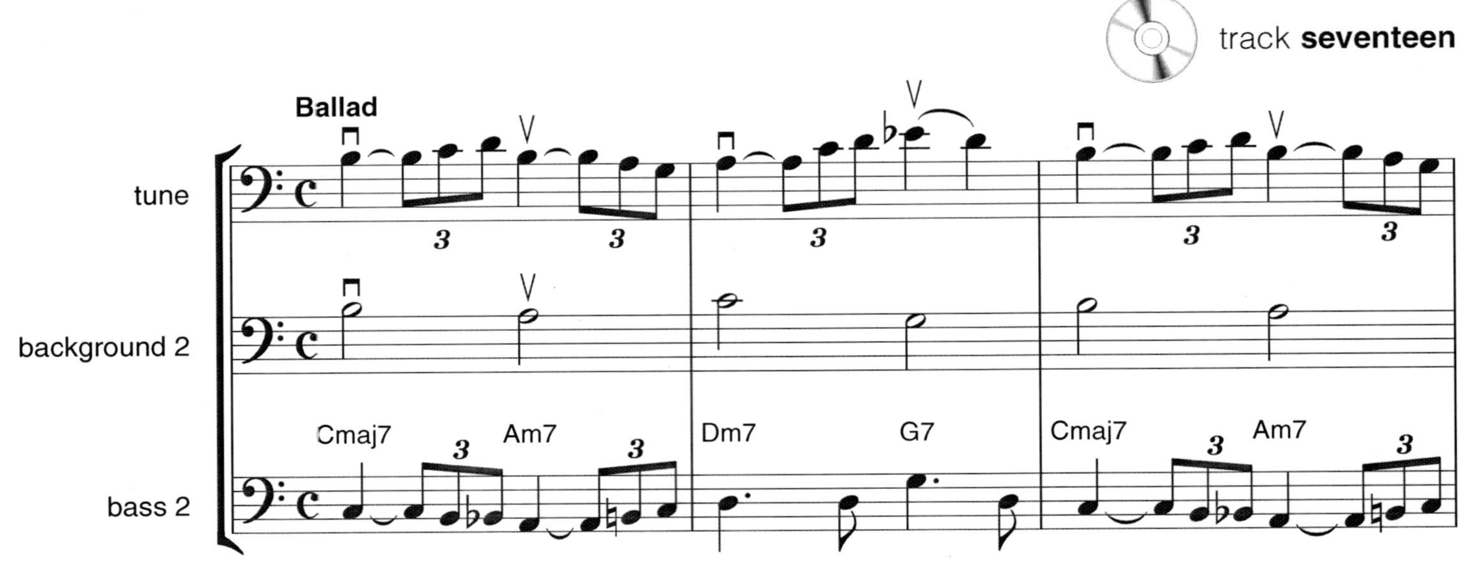

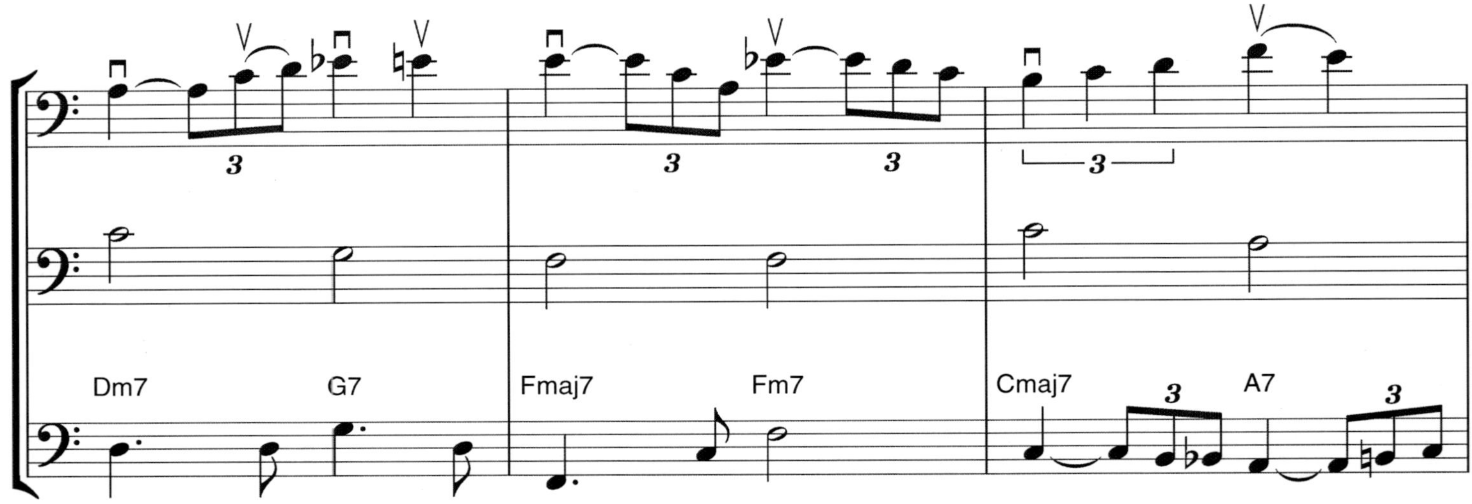

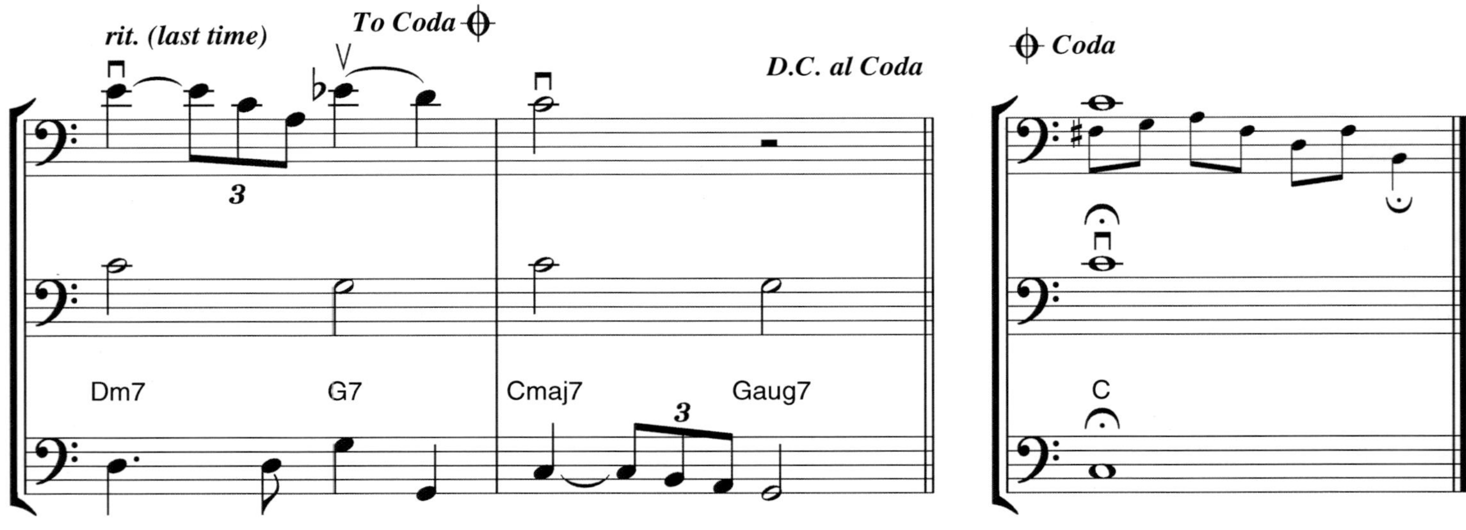

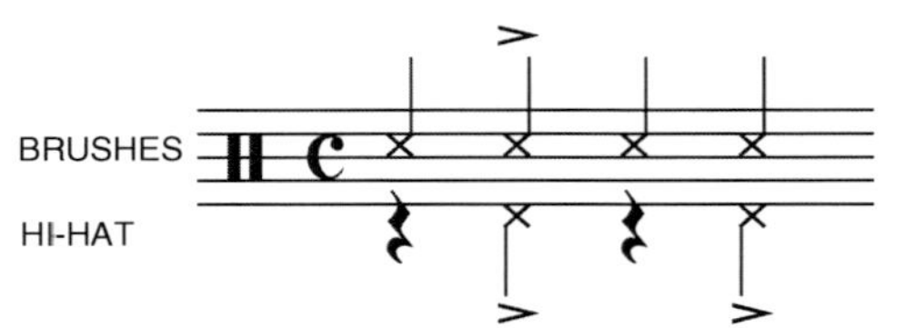

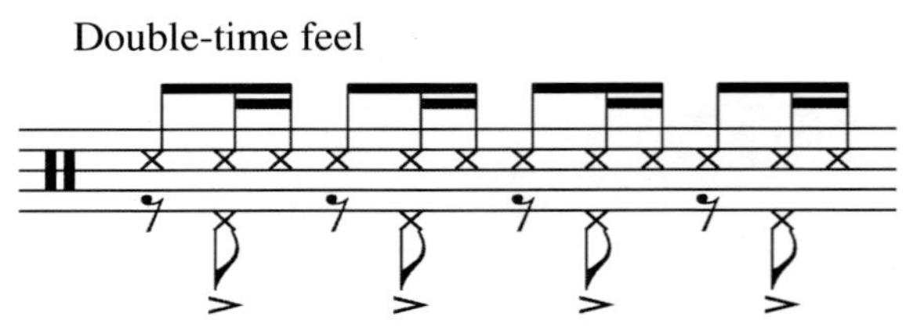

taking it slow solos

Ballad

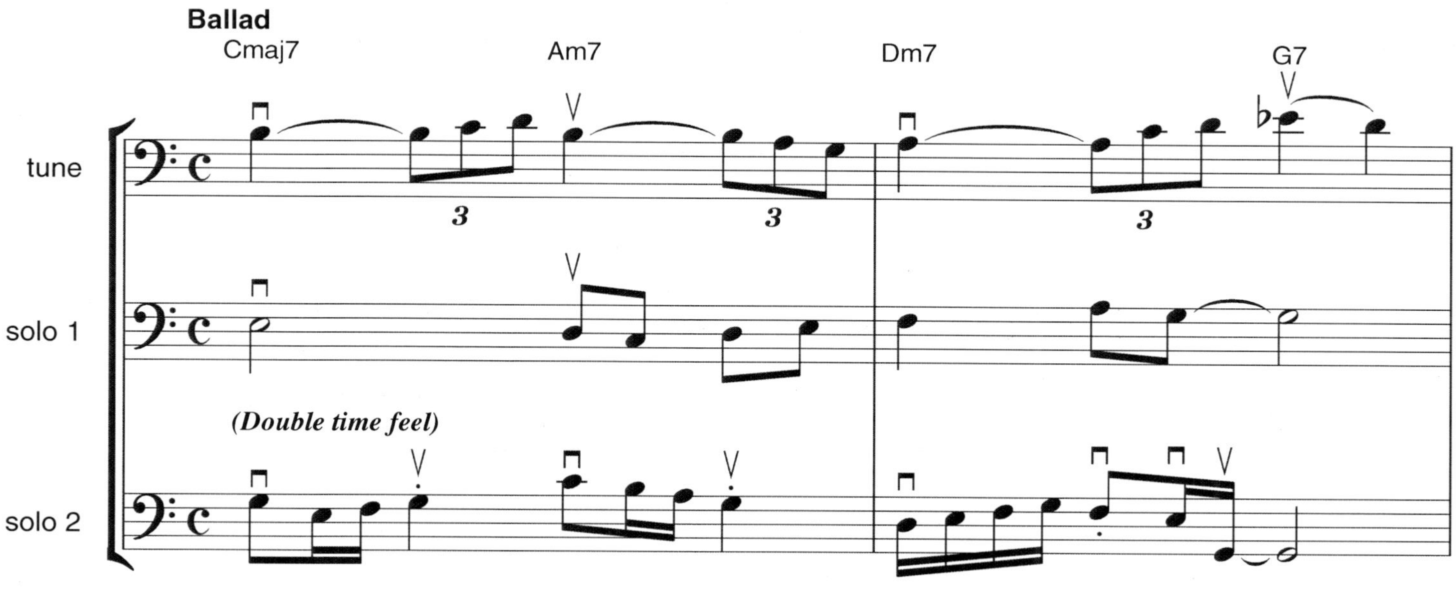

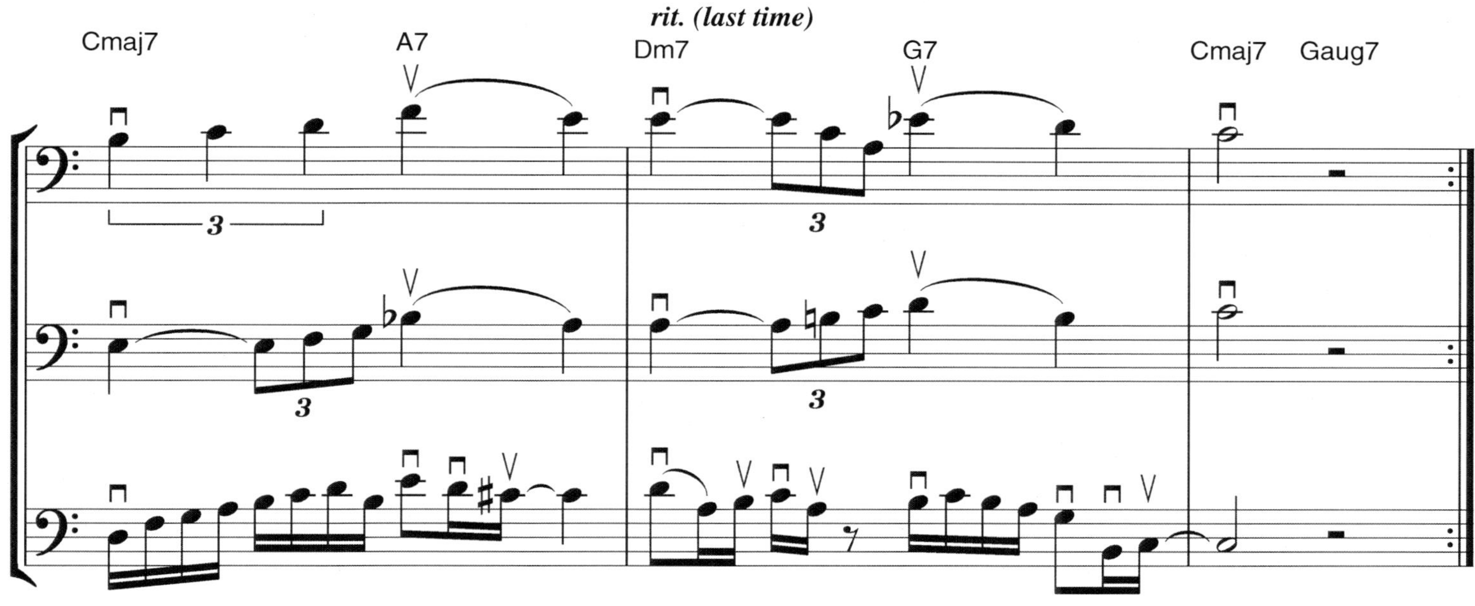

minor incident **preparatory pages**

CD: A jazz waltz ($\frac{3}{4}$ time) has a different feel to it than the traditional dance pulse found in the waltzes of Strauss. For example, instead of a heavy accent on beat 1 and a softer response on 2 and 3, the jazz waltz uses syncopation to create a light, bouncing feel (see drum pattern below). The Allman Brothers injected a hard driving blues-rock feel into a $\frac{3}{4}$ tune called "Hot 'Lanta." Their "Live at Fillmore East" recording is a classic example of brilliant "jamming."

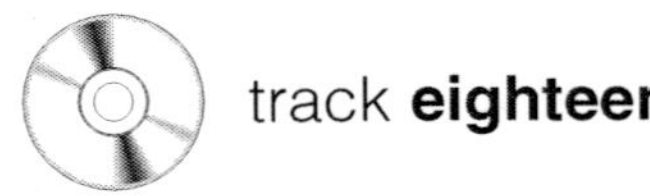

A Dorian Scale

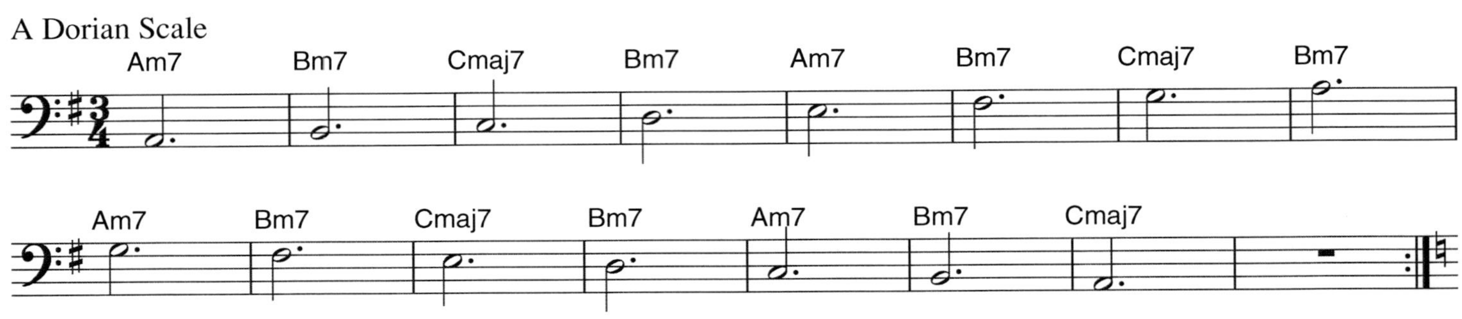

F Lydian Scale

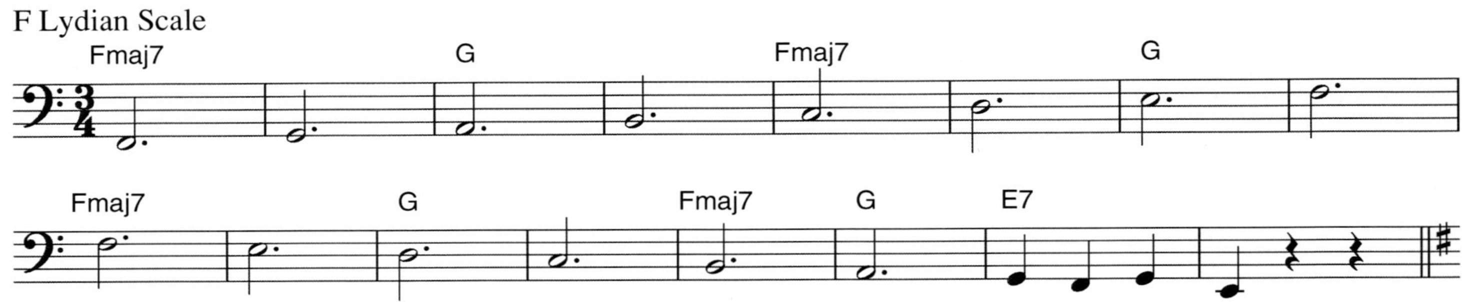

Two-Bar Rhythmic Echoes

Four-Bar Rhythmic Echoes

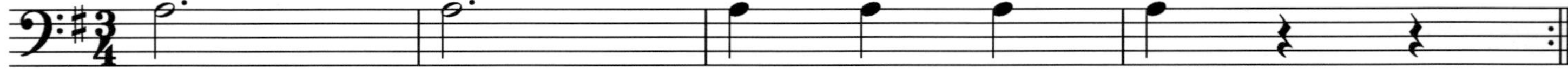

Improvisation Tip: The first 32 bars uses an A minor tonality. Dorian, blues, and harmonic minor can be blended giving you all these note choices: A, B, C, D, E♭, E, F, F♯, G, G♯. The last 16 bars involves a key change, therefore a new scale is required: an F major scale with a B♮ (Lydian mode), or a G major scale with an F♮ (Mixolydian mode). Either way you look at it, it's the same set of notes. Don't be afraid to use the G♮ on the E7, though you could choose a G♯ there as well. Then, switch back to A minor to start the chord progression over again, at the top.

Four-Bar Rhythmic Echoes

Two-Bar Melodic Echoes

Four-Bar Melodic Echoes

minor incident   tune and background

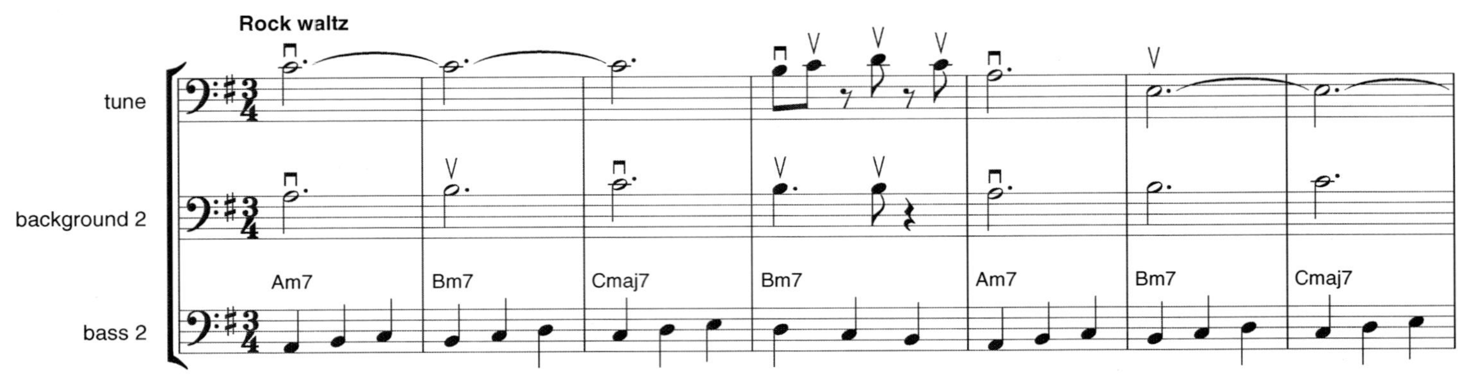

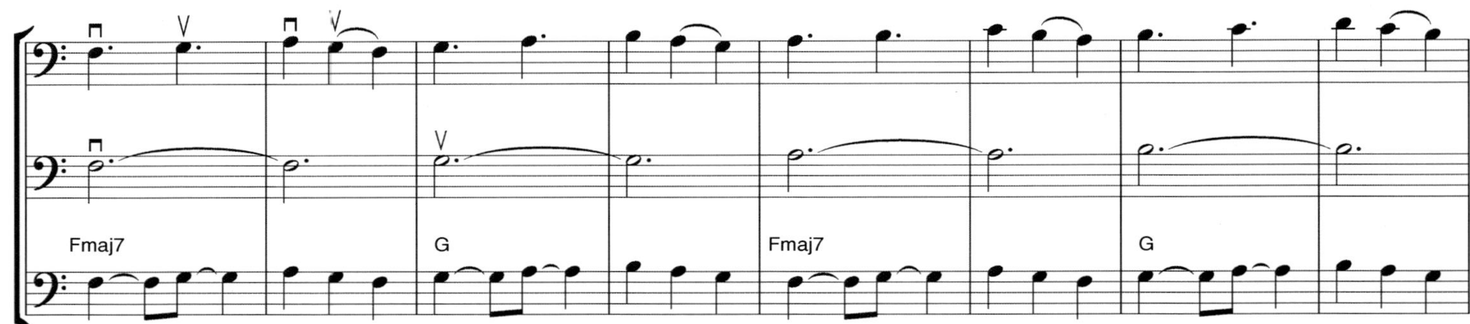

minor incident solos

who's the bossa? preparatory pages

CD: Antonio Carlos Jobim is one of the most well known composers of bossa nova and other Latin-style tunes. His compositions are famous for intricate rhythms, beautiful melodies and interesting (and therefore) challenging chord progressions. One of our favorites is "Wave."

Improvisation Tip: Improvising on this tune requires navigation through at least three different keys. The first 16 bars (8 measures repeated) could use only the C major scale or acknowledge the A⁷ to Dm⁷ with a C♯ and B♭ (D harmonic minor). The next 8-measure section is called the "bridge" and uses the F major scale for 4 bars, then the E♭ major scale for 3 bars. The last bar of the bridge uses a G⁷ chord to shift us back to the key of C for the remaining 8-bar section, which is the same as the first 8 measures of the tune. This is a common form called "AABA."

track **twenty**

You will notice a "strange" note in the second and sixth measures of the bridge: D♭ against a C^7 chord and B♮ against a $B♭^7$. These are called upper-structure notes and are colorful sounds added on top of a triad or seventh chord. Sometimes they are called "tension" notes for obvious reasons. This particular note is a flat 9. If you count the root (C) as 1 and go up the scale past the octave, D would be the ninth note. Lower it a half step to arrive at D♭, or the flat 9. In this case, a flat 9 adds a wonderful tension for a moment that then resolves by moving down a half step to the root. Include these notes in your scale as you weave your own melody through the chords.

One-Bar Rhythmic Echoes

Two-Bar Rhythmic Echoes

One-Bar Melodic Echoes

Two-Bar Melodic Echoes

who's the bossa? tune and background

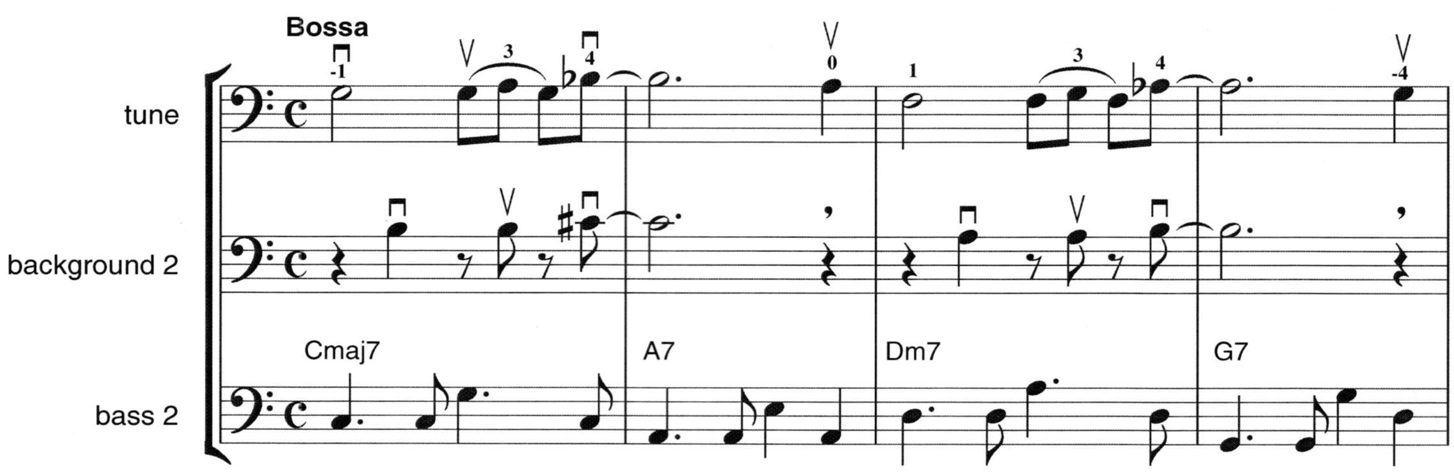

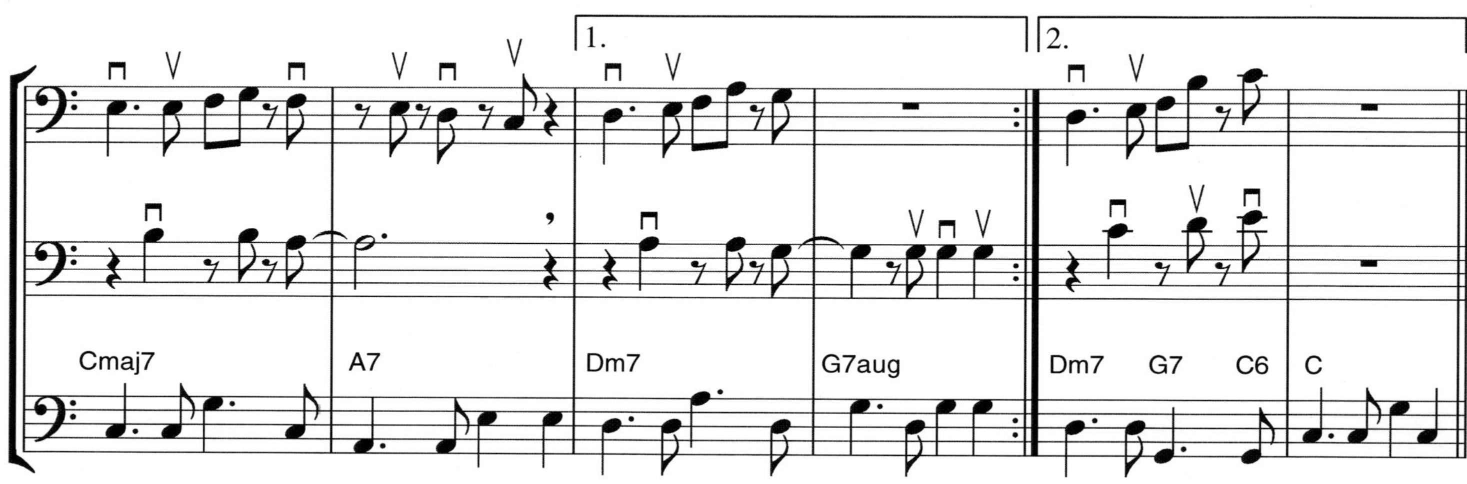

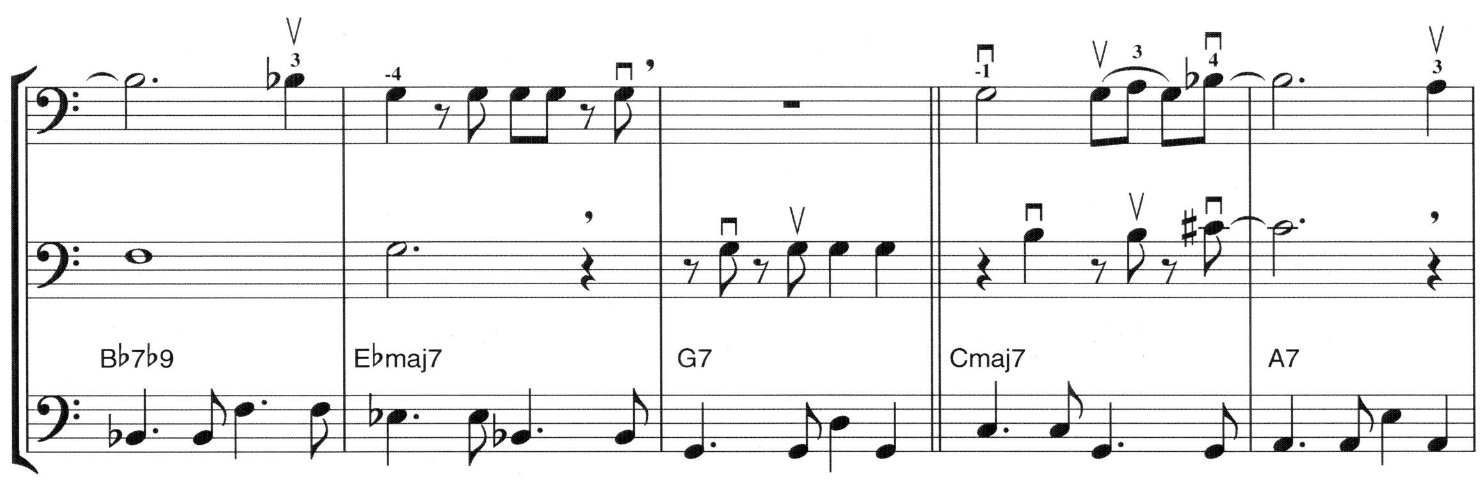
Bb7b9
Ebmaj7
G7
Cmaj7
A7

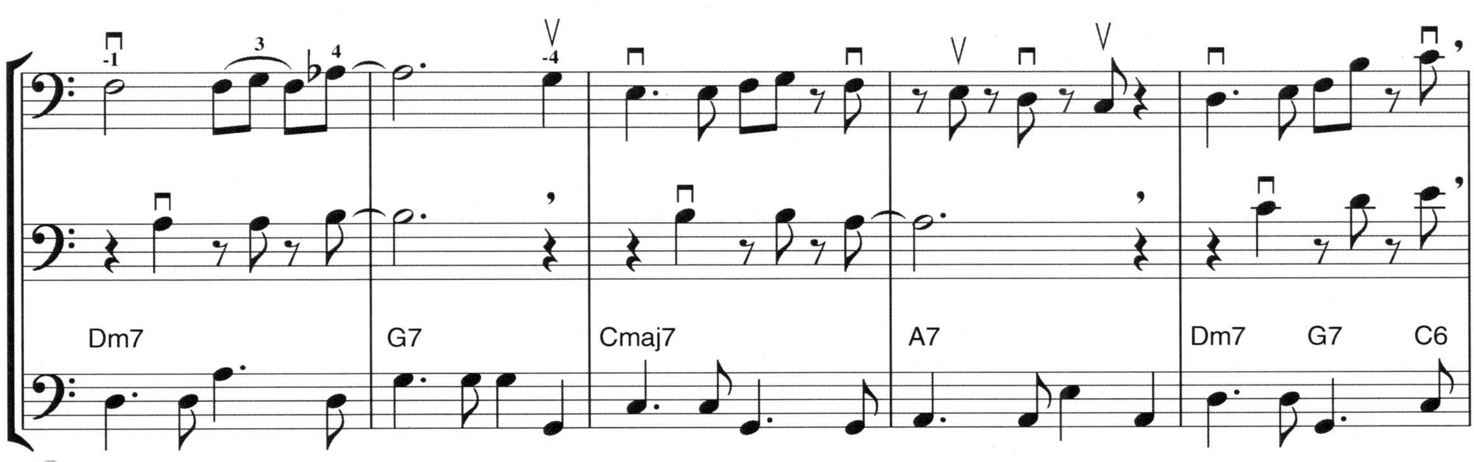
Dm7
G7
Cmaj7
A7
Dm7
G7
C6

D.C. al Coda, last
time To Coda
Coda
Dm7
G7
C
Dm7
G7
C6

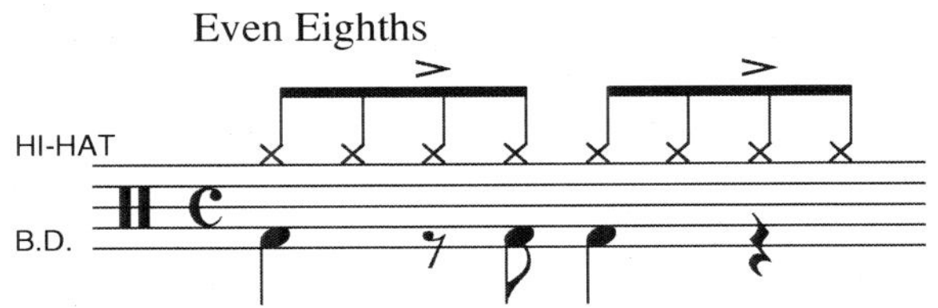
Even Eighths
HI-HAT
B.D.

36
who's the bossa solos
Bossa
tune
solo 1
solo 2
Cmaj7
A7
Dm7
G7
Cmaj7
A7
1.
Dm7
G7
2.
Dm7
G7
C
Gm7
C7
Fmaj7

Fm7
Bb7
Ebmaj7
G7
Cmaj7
A7
Dm7
G7
Cmaj7
A7
Dm7
G7
C6

boppin' along tune and background

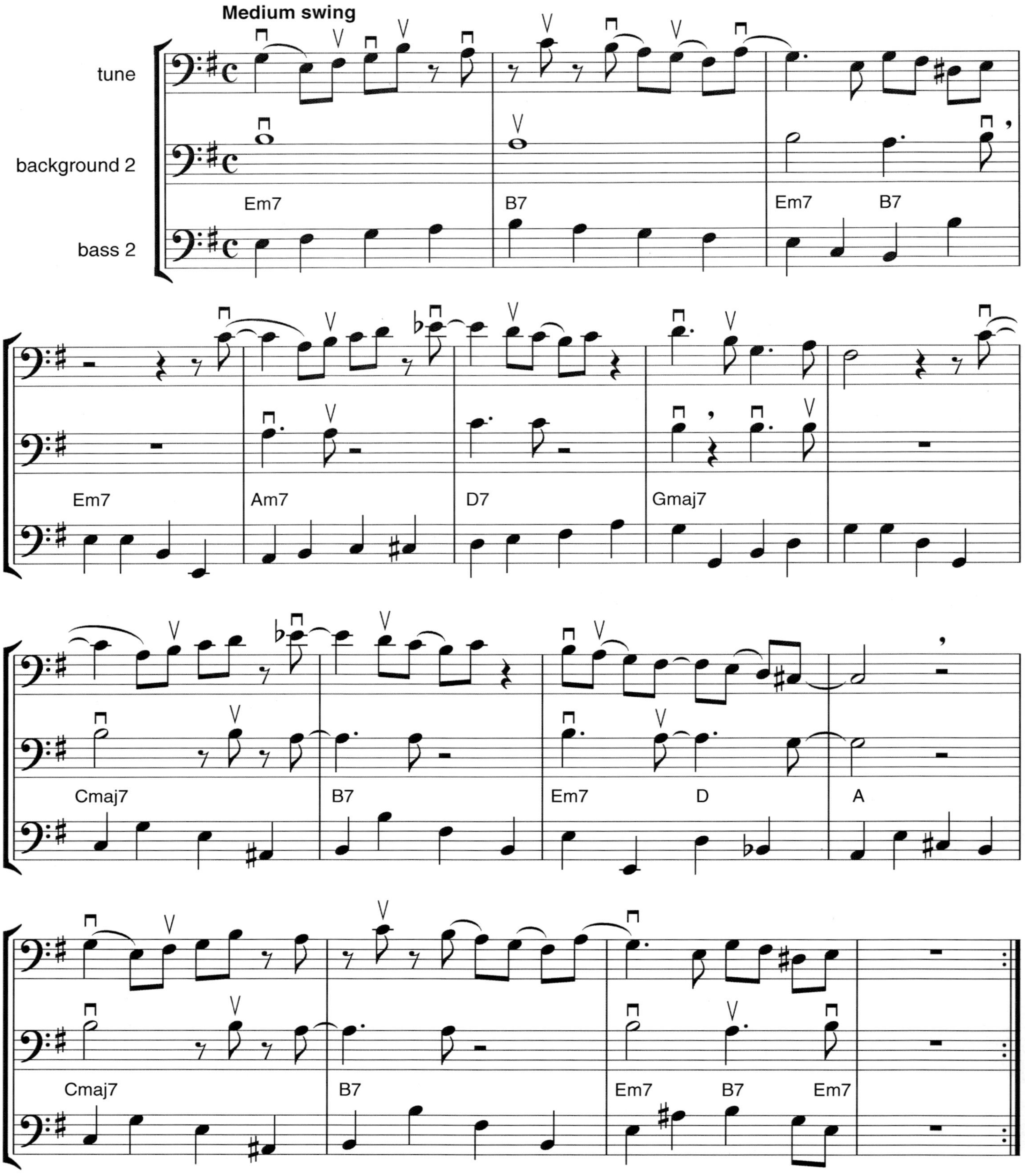

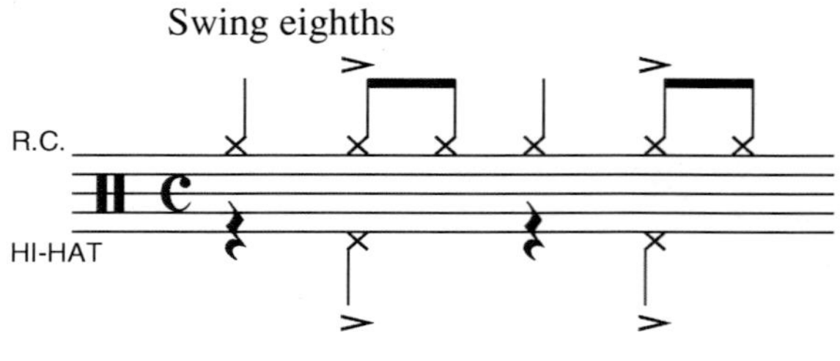

boppin' along solos

boppin' along   preparatory page

CD: Finding musicians to influence you doesn't need to be limited to the legendary jazz and blues players. David Grisman plays the mandolin and comes from a strong bluegrass background. He created his own style by blending bluegrass with jazz, using strings only (mandolin, violin, guitar and bass). Any of his recordings, especially the live concert with Stephane Grappelli, will inspire you. **Improvisation Tip:** You can successfully navigate through the entire tune using the E minor "be-bop" scale which uses both the raised 7th (D♯) and the lowered 7th (D♮). This works because E minor and G major share the same key signature. The only chord out of the key is A major in measure 12. Including a C♯ for one bar is the only alteration to make in the whole piece.

track **twenty-two**